BOOKS

Winchester, UK
Washington, USA

First published by John Hunt Publishing Ltd., 2001, 2003
Reprinted by O-Books 2010
O-Books is an imprint of John Hunt Publishing Ltd., Laurel House, Station Approach,
Alresford, Hants, SO24 9JH, UK
office1@o-books.net
www.o-books.com

For distributor details and how to order please visit the 'Ordering' section on
our website.

Text copyright: Andy Robb 2001

ISBN: 978 1 84694 386 7

Scriptures quoted from the Good News Bible published by The Bible
Societies/HarperCollins Publishers Ltd., UK.
© American Bible Society, 1966, 1971, 1976, 1992.

Design: Nautilus Design, UK
Illustrations: Andy Robb

Printed in the UK by CPI Antony Rowe
Printed in the USA by Offset Paperback Mfrs, Inc

We operate a distinctive and ethical publishing philosophy in
all areas of our business, from our global network of authors
to production and worldwide distribution.

CONTENTS

Introduction	5
God's Promises	10
Before Jesus's Birth	12
The Messiah Arrives	25
Jesus Growing Up	44
Jesus Aged 30	48
A Testing Time	52
Jesus's Miracles	63
Jesus's Teachings	71
Jesus Arrested	95
Jesus's Crucifixion	103
Risen From The Tomb	111
Jesus's Promises	115
The Bit At The End	121
Bitesize Bible Bits	123

Introduction

What's the most boring
thing you can think of?
Okay, now multiply it by
a zillion.
That's how boring a lot of
people think the Bible is.
The funny thing is, most
people who think the
Bible's mega mind-
numbingly boring have
never even read it!
Crazy or what?!

Imagine turning down a triple whopper chicken, cheese and
yoghurt burger with gherkin and custard relish just because
you'd never tried it...

On second thoughts that wasn't such a good suggestion.
But you get my point?
I mean, I'll bet you didn't even know that the Bible's got adverts
in it to tell people what's going to happen in the future or that
it told people that the world was round thousands of years
before we'd worked it out.
There's so much stuff in the Bible we won't be able to look at
every bit of it but the bits we've chosen will hopefully make you
start to realise that the Bible maybe isn't quite so boring as you
thought.
Have fun!

So What's The Bible All About?

The Bible isn't just one whopping great book.
It's actually 66 not-quite-so-whopping great books all whacked
together like a sort of mini library.

The first book in the Bible is called Genesis, which was also the name of a pop group your parents once liked but they won't admit to it even if you hang them from the ceiling by their toenails... and the last book is called Revelation which as far as I know wasn't the name of

a pop group your parents once liked.

To keep things simple, the Bible is mainly about two things.

God.
And people.

Some interesting questions.

Who exactly wrote the Bible?
People.

Who decided what to write about?
God.

So how did they know what God wanted them to write?
Did God send an e-mail?

Er, not quite.
Here's one way of looking at it.
Imagine two people in love.

Enough of that!
Sorry, have I put you off your lunch?
When people are in love with each other all they want to do is
spend every waking hour gazing lovingly into each other's eyes.
(I know, it's horrible, isn't it!)

The way they hug and cuddle each other you wonder whether they've been permanently super-glued to each other for all eternity.

It even gets to the point where they start to think each other's thoughts.

Well, that's sort of what it was like for the guys who wrote the Bible (without the cuddling bit).

They spent so much time with God that they got to know what he was thinking and what he wanted to say.

Sometimes God even spoke to them in dreams or gave them visions of what he wanted to say.

I THINK HIS EXCUSE THAT HE OVERSLEEPS SO THAT GOD CAN SPEAK TO HIM IN DREAMS IS WEARING A BIT THIN!

They were totally in touch with God so that what they wrote was as if God had written it himself.

So what sort of things does God want to say to us?

For starters, the Bible tells us that there is a God and that he made you and me and the whole universe.

It also tells us that he wants us to be his friends and how we can do that.

What good is a book that was written *even before* my mum and dad were born? People might not wear silly costumes like they did in the past but God hasn't changed a bit, so what he had to say to people with funny headdresses and sandals thousands of years ago is still important for us.

This Boring Bible book's taken mainly from four books in the *New* Testament bit of the Bible.
They are **MATTHEW, MARK, LUKE** and **JOHN**.
But they all tell the story of one man...God's *Super Son*.

(By the way, I was only joking about hanging your parents upside down by their toenails - nose hairs work much better!!!)

Here's a question for you.

Would you marry someone you'd never met before?
(Okay, so I know you're not old enough to marry yet, but just answer the question anyway!)

The chances are your answer's going to be something like this...

You'll probably have heard stories in the news about couples who 'date' on the internet and then meet up, face to face, for the first time at their wedding!
But what if they don't like the look of each other?

It's a bit late to change your mind when the church is packed full of well-wishers.

It's like at Christmas when Auntie so-and-so has promised you something really special but when you rip off the wrapping paper it's nothing like you imagined it would be, so you go off in a sulk.

This Boring Bible book is all about some people who'd *also* been promised a mega special Christmas pressie but when they took a second look at it they figured it wasn't really what they'd been hoping for at all.
In fact, they were so mad that they hadn't got what they wanted that they went and chucked it out.

Just in case you haven't read any of the other Boring Bible books (shame on you!), it won't be a bad idea if we quickly check out some of the stuff that's been going on *before Super Son*.

COUNTDOWN TO SUPER SON

10 God creates the world.

9 God makes people.

8 People disobey God.

7 The friendship between God and people is destroyed.

6 People forget all about God and become more and more wicked.

5 But God doesn't forget about people.

4 God chooses Abraham to start the Israelite nation.

3 The Israelites' job is to remind people what God is like and that he still loves them.

2 That's too tough an order even for the Israelites.

1 God is now going to send a very special Israelite who will finish the job, once and for all. The Israelites call him the Messiah and when he comes, hey, won't everyone know it!

WE HAVE LIFT OFF !

If you hadn't guessed already, *Super Son* is all about **Jesus**.

Now, on the one hand you might well know more than a thing or two about Jesus.

On the other hand you might not have the teeniest idea who he was.

Have no fear, the Boring Bible book has come to the rescue!

But first, to the small matter of the Israelites' whom we've left patiently waiting for their Messiah.

Boring Bible Fact: A Messiah was someone God had chosen to do a special job for him.

As time passed, and there was *still* no sign of the Messiah, the Israelites started to come up with their own ideas of what he was going to be like.

They were getting particularly cheesed off that the land they lived in was ruled by the Romans.

As far as the Israelites were concerned they were looking for a Messiah who would send the Romans packing with a flea in their ear.

Unfortunately, this wasn't quite what God had in mind but more of that later.

First, let's find out what on earth those rotten Romans were doing in Israel making life so beastly for the Jewish people.

The Rotten Romans

If there was one thing the Romans enjoyed above most other things it was a spot of good old conquering.

If a nation decided to put its feet up for five minutes and relax then...

BAM!

...in charged the Romans to conquer them.

To be fair, they were pretty good at it but that's not the point! You'd think that they'd be content with just having a small or even a regular-sized empire, but nothing of the sort.

The sort of empire the Romans wanted was extra large with fries on the side.

This was bad news for the Israelites.

Things hadn't been going very well for them for quite some time and the last thing *they* needed was to be invaded by the Romans.

If you've read Boring Bible book *Catastrophic Kings* then you'll be well aware what a botch the Israelites often made of things (but then, don't we all!).

God had been incredibly patient with them (like he is with us) but they *still* kept on disobeying him.

Enough was enough and God finally called time on their rebellious ways by allowing Israel to be conquered and the Israelites to be taken away as slaves to foreign lands.

Although God eventually let them return to Israel, from then on they had to put up with a succession of invading armies wanting to conquer them.

First it was the Greeks...

Then the Syrians...

And finally the Romans.

Fascinating Fact:

The Greek (or Macedonian) army was led by none other than the famous Alexander the Great. He decided that everyone in his massive empire should speak the same language - Greek. That's why the New Testament part of the Bible was written in Greek. It was the language that most people could read and write in.

The Romans weren't daft.
To prevent the Jewish people from feeling too down-trodden they allowed them to have their own king, Herod.
How kind.
But, to tell the truth, Herod was nothing more than a puppet king who did exactly as he was told.

I wonder how *you'd* feel if another family came and lived with you in your house without being invited?

a Couldn't care less.

b Mildly annoyed.

c Very annoyed.

d Very, very annoyed.

e Very, very, very annoyed.

f So teeth-gnashingly angry you feel like you want to throw them out the bedroom window whether it's open or not!

If you answered f) then that's roughly how the Israelites felt about having the Romans come and live in their patch of land except for the bit about the bedroom window.

Bedroom windows hadn't been invented yet.

As far as the Jewish people were concerned, the sooner the Romans cleared off back to Rome the better.

They were fed up having to pay heaps and heaps of taxes to the Romans just for the privilege of having them rule over them.

And it was totally out of order for the Romans to crucify anybody who dared to stir up trouble against them.

If only God would send them a great leader like Moses (check out Boring Bible book *Magnificent Moses* for more info) then he could lead them to victory and they could run Israel like back in the good old days.

Boring Bible Joke: Why didn't the Israelites use Jewish measurements?
Because they had Roman *rulers*!

But God had other ideas.
You see, God wasn't just planning to rescue the Israelites, he was going to rescue *everybody*.

Let me explain...

God's Great Big Rescue Plan

Right from the time Adam and Eve spoiled things between people and God (they were the world's first two people - take a look in Boring Bible book *Ballistic Beginnings* if you don't believe me!) God had it in his heart to patch things up with humans.

Just one problem! Something was getting in the way.

The Bible calls what people did by turning their backs on God and doing bad things, 'sin'.

And sin is what comes between us and God.

If we do something wrong like rob a bank or beat someone up there's a good chance we'll end up in front of a judge.

Like it or not, we're going to get punished for what we've done.
Every crime (or sin) that's ever been committed against God
since Adam and Eve's first sin of disobeying God (right up to all
the sins that are happening right now as you read this book),
has got to be punished.

Good point!
Now let me ask *you* a question.
On second thoughts, here's a story for you to read, *then* I'll ask
the question...

Okay, now here's the question I promised you.

What was wrong with the teacher's decision?

Yep, you got it!

He wasn't **fair**.

And the Bible says that God is always 100% fair.
If God *didn't* punish people for doing wrong then he *wouldn't* be fair.
Can you imagine a judge picking and choosing who he punished and who he didn't depending what sort of mood he was in?
It would be a complete disaster.

The bottom line is that sin *has* to be punished.
If it's not, then there's zilcho chance of people and God *ever* getting back together again.
The trouble is, according to the Bible, there's absolutely nothing that *we* can do about it.
So, it's not only the Israelites who need a Messiah...
we **all** do!

SITUATIONS VACANT

WANTED: **MESSIAH**. MUST BE ABLE TO WORK WELL WITH GOD AND WITH PEOPLE. MUST HAVE **NO** PREVIOUS EXPERIENCE OF SIN. MAIN JOB TASK IS TO SORT OUT SIN. SOME TEACHING INVOLVED. LONG HOURS. **LOW PAY**. SHORT LIFE. APPLICATIONS SHOULD BE IN BEFORE THE BEGINNING OF TIME.

Because God is God, he knew even before he'd created the world that it would need a Messiah.

Now, at long last, the time had finally come for him to be revealed.

A Beginners' Guide To Spotting A Messiah

History is littered with people claiming to be a Messiah sent from God so it's not always easy to spot a real one from a fake. Here are a few handy hints to help you make up your own mind.

1 Did you get any advance warning that they were on their way?
   If they *were* a Messiah from God he'd give you plenty of notice of the fact so you didn't miss them.
2 Did anybody else back up their story that they were the Messiah?
   A few angels announcing the fact or the odd voice from heaven wouldn't go amiss.
3 Did they do anything out of the ordinary to prove that they'd been sent by God?

Whenever you see this **SPOT THE MESSIAH** logo anywhere in this book you can use these three handy checks to see whether Jesus really *was* the **real thing**.

Okay, now on with the story.
The Bible features two
accounts of how the Messiah
arrived.

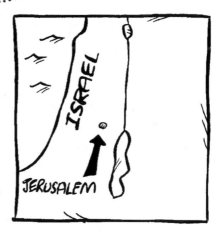

Some of the bits overlap but
when you put them together
you get the whole story.
It doesn't actually kick off
with Jesus but with some of
his relatives who lived near to
Israel's capital city, Jerusalem.

That's because the dad, Zechariah worked as a priest in the
Temple.
Up to then Zechariah and his wife Elizabeth were childless and,
according to the Bible, they were getting on a bit.

Once a year, one of the priests had the awesome job of going
right into the heart of the Temple where God was.
This year it fell to Zechariah.
In went old Zechariah but the sight that met his eyes nearly had
him leaping out of his sandals.

DON'T BE AFRAID, ZECHARIAH! GOD HAS HEARD YOUR PRAYER. YOUR WIFE ELIZABETH **WILL** HAVE A SON. YOU WILL NAME HIM JOHN. HE WILL GET PEOPLE READY FOR GOD'S ARRIVAL.

It was an angel from God.

HOW CAN I BELIEVE THAT? MY WIFE AND I ARE BOTH **OLD**?!

Bad move, Zechariah...

> I AM GABRIEL. I STAND IN THE PRESENCE OF GOD WHO SENT ME TO SPEAK TO YOU. BECAUSE YOU HAVEN'T BELIEVED MY MESSAGE, YOU WILL BE UNABLE TO SPEAK UNTIL THE DAY MY PROMISE COMES TRUE!

...said the angel.

The *good* news was that Zechariah's old wife, Elizabeth, really did fall pregnant but more of that in a bit.

Meanwhile, about 60 miles away, in a town called Nazareth...

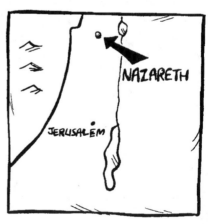

...the angel Gabriel was getting ready to make *another* surprise visit.

This time he was delivering a message from God to a girl called Mary who was shortly to be married to a guy called Joseph.

> PEACE BE WITH YOU! ...

...said the angel.
Mary was anything but peaceful.
She was well shocked.

> DON'T BE AFRAID, MARY, GOD HAS BEEN GRACIOUS TO YOU. YOU WILL BECOME PREGNANT AND GIVE BIRTH TO A SON AND YOU WILL NAME HIM JESUS. HE WILL BE GREAT AND WILL BE CALLED THE SON OF THE MOST HIGH GOD. THE LORD GOD WILL BE KING OF THE DESCENDANTS OF JACOB FOR EVER. HIS KINGDOM WILL NEVER END!

Mary was amazed.

But God was well aware of that...

THE HOLY SPIRIT WILL COME ON YOU AND GOD'S POWER WILL REST ON YOU. FOR THIS REASON THE HOLY CHILD WILL BE CALLED THE **SON OF GOD**.

SPOT THE MESSIAH We've got an angel here to give us our first clue that Jesus was someone special sent from God!

Mary was more trusting than Zechariah and believed every word the angel said.

Boring Bible Fact: To have a baby before you were married would have been a terrible thing in Mary's day. Such was the disgrace it brought upon the family that often the girl was killed as a punishment.

The Bible tells us that Joseph, the man Mary was engaged to, didn't want to disgrace Mary publicly so he made plans to break off the engagement privately.
Before he'd had the chance to act, Joseph also had a surprise visitor, but this time it was in a dream.

Yep, you guessed it...it was an angel!

> JOSEPH! DON'T BE AFRAID TO TAKE MARY AS YOUR WIFE. IT IS BY THE HOLY SPIRIT THAT SHE HAS FALLEN PREGNANT. SHE WILL HAVE A SON AND YOU WILL NAME HIM **JESUS** BECAUSE HE WILL SAVE PEOPLE FROM THEIR SINS.

SPOT THE MESSIAH *Another* angel and some more info about the sort of person the Messiah's going to be.

As far as Joseph was concerned there was no arguing with an angel from God.

The Bible says that when Joseph woke up he married Mary.

Er, well perhaps it wasn't *quite* like that.

Just in case you were wondering what had happened to poor old dumb-struck Zechariah, let me quickly fill you in.

As promised, Elizabeth gave birth to a boy.

Traditionally the baby took either the father's name or the name of a relative.

When Zechariah was asked what the baby's name was to be, he wrote down on a writing tablet exactly what the angel had told him...

At that moment he was able to speak again.

All their friends and neighbours were awestruck.

It was plain to them that this child was going to be someone special.

And in a bit we're going to discover just how right they were.

Count Me In

If you're anything like my kids you'll just love spreading out all your hard-saved pocket money to count every last penny so you know precisely how much you've got.

Every few years many countries do their own bit of totting up only it's not money they're counting but *people*.

Not only do they want to know how many people they've got but lots of other facts and figures about them as well.

The Romans were no exception.

With such a vast empire it was important that the people back in Rome knew who and what they were ruling.

Just before Jesus was born, the Roman Emperor Augustus ordered a census to be taken.

In those days you couldn't just fill in your census form and pop it in the post.

You had to register yourself where your ancestors came from, which in Joseph's case was Bethlehem.

The Bible doesn't tell us how long it took Mary and Joseph to travel from Nazareth to Bethlehem but it can't have been a comfortable journey especially as Mary was soon to give birth. Things didn't get much better on their arrival in Bethlehem. It might have been a small town but the place would have been swarming with people who'd *also* gone there to register for the census.

With the clock ticking away to Jesus's birth, Mary and Joseph must have started to panic when they couldn't find anywhere to stay.

Fascinating Fact:

Most versions of the Bible say that Mary and Joseph couldn't find room in an inn and that the baby Jesus was laid in a cattle trough or manger. A better translation would be 'upper room' not inn, which makes sense when you discover that in the hills round Bethlehem people still live in caves along with their animals. The upper room bit of the cave is where the people live and on the lower floor they keep their animals. If the upper room had been full up then sleeping down below with the animals would have been better than nothing!

You might well be wondering what on earth God was playing at allowing his own Son to be born alongside all those smelly cattle rather than in a grand palace somewhere, but as we've already seen in the other Boring Bible books, the way *God* does things and the way *we* do things are completely different.

As was the tradition in those days, Mary wrapped her newborn baby in strips of cloth. Jewish mothers believed that this would make the baby's limbs grow straight.

Just like the angel had told him, Joseph called the boy 'Jesus'.

Boring Bible Fact: The name Jesus means 'God is salvation' or 'Saviour' which gives us a rather big clue as to what Jesus had been sent by God to do.

Meanwhile, out in the fields surrounding Bethlehem, some sleepy shepherds were about to get the shock of their lives...

DON'T BE AFRAID! I AM HERE WITH GOOD NEWS WHICH WILL BRING JOY TO ALL THE PEOPLE. THIS VERY DAY, IN DAVID'S TOWN, YOUR SAVIOUR WAS BORN – CHRIST THE LORD! AND THIS IS WHAT WILL PROVE IT TO YOU. YOU WILL FIND A BABY WRAPPED IN STRIPS OF CLOTH, LYING IN A MANGER!

Before they'd had a chance to recover, the whole sky was filled with angels praising God.

The shepherds didn't need telling twice.

They hot-footed it to Bethlehem and found Jesus just like they'd been told.

SPOT THE MESSIAH A whole *sky-full* of angels this time just in case that there was any doubt that Jesus was the Messiah!

Although our calendars are based around the year of Jesus's birth they are, in fact, all wrong by about four years.

It's all down to a guy called Dionysius Exiguus but you can call him 'Ex' because if all the calendar makers get their hands on him that's what he's going to be...an *Ex*-Dionysius!

He was a sixth-century abbot who got his facts and figures in a bit of a mess and miscalculated the date of Jesus's birth.

So what we are left with is Jesus being born in 4BC (BC means 'Before Christ') which sounds strange...but completely true!

Because Mary and Joseph were obedient Jews they made a special trip up to Jerusalem to dedicate Jesus to God and to perform a purification ceremony for the child, which was required by Jewish law.

While they were there, not one, but *two* weird things happened to them.

First, a man called Simeon approached them and, taking Jesus in his arms, said...

Simeon was a man who loved God.

God had promised Simeon that he would not die until he had seen God's promised Messiah.

SPOT THE MESSIAH Simeon backs up the evidence that Jesus really is God's promised Messiah.

Would you believe it but within an hour of Simeon's little speech along comes an old lady called Anna and *she* starts to tell everyone waiting for Israel's Messiah all about Jesus as well.

A Wise Move

If Mary and Joseph thought that was it for visitors and well-wishers then they had another think coming.

Far, far away in the East, wise men who specialised in studying the movements of the stars had spotted an unusual star.

To them it pointed to the birth of a king.

With their bags packed they headed off in hot pursuit. It led them to Jerusalem where they made further enquiries about Israel's newborn king.

News of the wise men reached King Herod's ears and he called together all the religious leaders and teachers to see what they had to say.

Sneaky Herod sent the wise men off to do his dirty work and find out whether this really *was* true.

Don't be fooled by Herod's sweet words.
He had no intention of worshipping this new king.
As far as he was concerned there was only room for one king in Israel and that was *him*.
Herod only wanted to find out where Jesus was so he could have him killed.

The Bible says that the wise men continued to follow the star all the way to Bethlehem where it stopped over the place where the child was.

Boring Bible Interesting Thought: How could a star stop over just one specific house? If you look up at the starry sky, a particular star might lead you to a region or maybe even a city but not an actual house. Could this star have been something that *looked* like a shining star but was really an angel? After all, angels appeared to everyone else so why not to the wise men? *There's* something for you to think about!

When *my* children were born they got lots of lovely presents from family and friends.
Babygros, bibs, cuddly toys. You name it, we got it.
The wise men were no exception, but the gifts they brought for Jesus were a bit out of the ordinary to say the least.
They brought gold, frankincense and myrrh!
Gold for a king.
Incense for God.
And myrrh for mortal man.

SPOT THE MESSIAH God had said that the Messiah would be born in Bethlehem and sure enough that's exactly where he was born!

Imagine Mary and Joseph's surprise when these visitors from the East knelt down and worshipped Jesus.
Even these wise men recognised that this baby was someone out of the ordinary.
And as far as going back to nasty old Herod with the baby's whereabouts, well he never heard from the wise men again.
God had warned them in a dream not to go back to him so they went home by another route.

Boring Bible Fact: People always talk about the *three* wise men but the Bible never says how many of them there were. All it tells us is that there were *three gifts*.

It wasn't only the wise men who got a warning from God. Shortly afterwards, an angel from God appeared to Joseph and said...

HEROD IS LOOKING FOR THE CHILD IN ORDER TO KILL HIM, SO GET UP, TAKE THE CHILD AND HIS MOTHER AND ESCAPE TO EGYPT AND STAY THERE UNTIL I TELL YOU TO LEAVE.

At the dead of night, Mary and Joseph fled to Egypt.

It wasn't long before Herod realised that he'd been well and truly tricked by the wise men.
He was furious!

Herod thought that this would make certain that the baby king was destroyed before he had a chance to become a threat to him.
How wrong he was.
Sadly, many little boys were needlessly killed by this tyrannical ruler because Jesus was already well out of harm's way, somewhere in Egypt.

Only once Herod had died did an angel from God give Joseph the all-clear to return to Israel.

Unfortunately, the next Herod, Archelaus, was just as bad as his father.
Going back to Bethlehem in Judea with *another* nasty piece of work as king was not a good idea.
In a dream, God instructed Joseph to head for Nazareth in Galilee and that's where Jesus grew up.

How Frustrating!!!

Would you believe it?!

The Bible tells us almost nothing at all about Jesus growing up. All we've got is a three-day snippet when he was twelve and then we have to wait until he's 30 before we hear any more from him.

What I'd Like To Know Is...

1 Did Jesus *know* he was the Son of God when he was a child?
2 What did it feel like being God and a boy at the same time?
3 Did his family treat him any different?
4 Was he popular?
5 Did he do what he was told?
6 Was he a fussy eater?
7 Did he do his homework?
8 Did he get pocket money?
9 Did he keep his room tidy?
10 Was he fun to be with?

What do *you* think?

Here's what the Bible says happened to Jesus when he was twelve...

So, there's a clue that even when he was twelve, Jesus was well aware that *God* in heaven was his *real* Father.

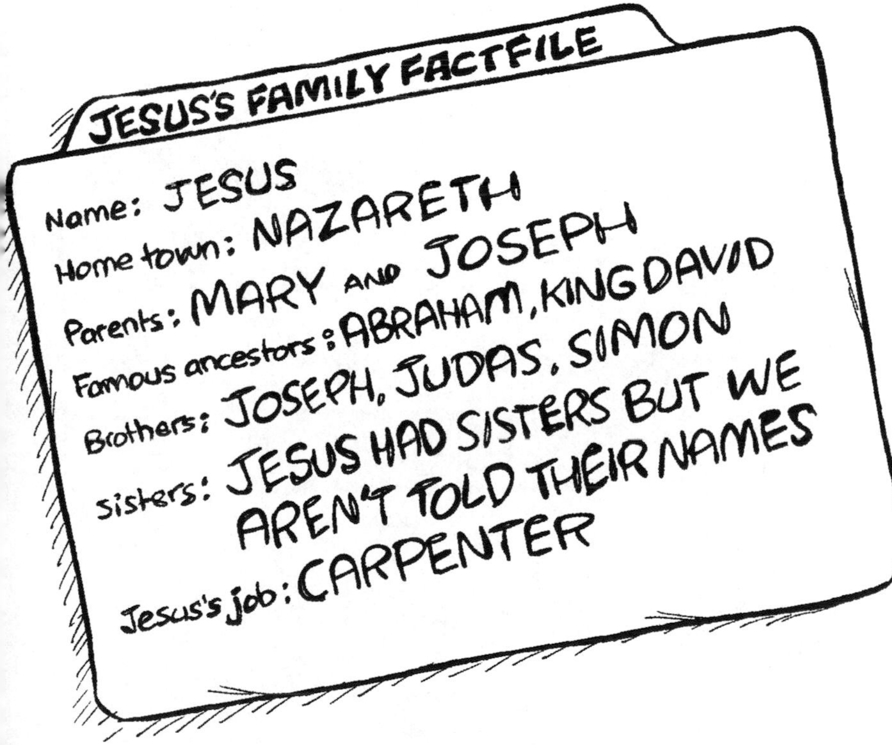

JESUS'S FAMILY FACTFILE

Name: JESUS

Home town: NAZARETH

Parents: MARY AND JOSEPH

Famous ancestors: ABRAHAM, KING DAVID

Brothers: JOSEPH, JUDAS, SIMON

Sisters: JESUS HAD SISTERS BUT WE AREN'T TOLD THEIR NAMES

Jesus's job: CARPENTER

Okay. let's fast forward a few years.

Jesus is now about 30 years old and life is about to change for ever.

Time to get re-aquainted with someone else who's gone and got all grown up.

REMEMBER ME? **JOHN!** YOU KNOW... ZECHARIAH'S BOY!

It was no coincidence John being born around the same time as Jesus.

And it wasn't only Jesus who'd got a special job from God...*John* had as well.

John's job was to announce that Jesus, the Super Son, was on his way...

OKAY, EVERYONE, I WANT YOU TO PUT YOUR HANDS TOGETHER AND GIVE A BIG NAZARETH WELCOME TO...

Not *that* sort of announcer!
This sort of announcer...

That's more like it.

SPOT THE MESSIAH God sent John to back up Jesus's claim to be the Messiah!

John's job was to show the Israelites that they needed to turn away from their wicked lives and turn to God.
And John used a brilliant visual aid to help them do it.
He got people to be baptised in the River Jordan which ran through the desert.
The Israelites were plunged under the water to represent the death of their wicked lives, the washing away of all traces of sin and then coming out of the water to a clean, fresh start with God.
That's how John got the nickname...**John the Baptist**.

Then one day, *Jesus* showed up.

Hang on a minute!

The Bible says that Jesus never, ever sinned. He was **perfect**.

So, what's he doing getting baptised then?

The answer is that Jesus was going to be the sort of Messiah who led by example.

If Jesus wanted people to listen to him he had to show them that he wasn't proud and aloof but humble and caring.

Okay, I want you to put your Sherlock Holmes detective hats on because in a moment there's going to be a whopping big 'SPOT THE MESSIAH' clue and I want you to see if *you* can spot it.
Here goes with more of the story.

Did you spot it?
You're right! God's voice speaking from heaven.
Awesome!

The dove represented God's Holy Spirit coming down onto Jesus.
Filled with the Holy Spirit of God, Jesus was now ready for action.
At long last, God's great big plan to patch things up with people had begun.

A Testing Time

Most things you buy from the shops have at some time been tested.

If you've got a skateboard it's probably been tested to make sure that the wheels don't fall off just when you're about to go round a sharp bend at top speed.

Computers need to be tested to make sure they can do all the amazing things the manufacturers promise they can.

Even headache pills you take after you've fallen off your skateboard or spent too long on your PC need to be tested out before they hit the shops.

Not surprisingly, before Jesus was allowed by his Father in heaven to go out and do his stuff with the Israelites, he had to be *tested* to make sure he was up to it.

If something's going to be tested then you're going to need a tester.

The tester Jesus had was God's No.1 enemy, the devil or Satan. (If you want some more info on him then check out Boring Bible book, *Ballistic Beginnings*.)

Jesus, God's Super Son, had been sent on a mission from God to undo the damage that Satan had done to his wonderful world so, first off, it was important to see whether Jesus was going to be able to pull the whole thing off.

The Bible says that God's Holy Spirit led Jesus out into the desert where he got himself ready.

For 40 days Jesus didn't eat a thing.

Now the testing time had arrived.

WELCOME TO THE GREATEST BATTLE OF ALL TIME! IT'S A THREE-ROUND CONTEST AND IF **JESUS** WINS, THEN THE HUMAN RACE IS IN WITH A CHANCE. IF **SATAN** WINS EVEN JUST **ONE** ROUND, IT'S CURTAINS FOR US ALL! SECONDS AWAY, ROUND ONE...

IF YOU ARE GOD'S SON THEN TURN THE STONES INTO BREAD!

THE BIBLE SAYS THAT MAN DOES NOT LIVE ON BREAD ALONE BUT ON EVERY WORD THAT COMES FROM THE MOUTH OF GOD.

THAT'S ROUND ONE TO JESUS. WE'RE NOW SWITCHING LOCATIONS TO JERUSALEM. IF YOU'RE SCARED OF HEIGHTS THEN LOOK AWAY **NOW**! SECONDS AWAY, ROUND TWO...

IF YOU ARE THE SON OF GOD, THROW YOURSELF DOWN BECAUSE THE BIBLE SAYS THAT GOD WILL COMMAND HIS ANGELS TO LOOK AFTER YOU!

IT IS **ALSO** WRITTEN, THAT YOU SHOULDN'T PUT GOD TO THE TEST.

Jesus had passed the test with flying colours...

Jesus was now ready to roll.
There was so much that had to be done but so little time.
Only *Jesus* knew that he now had just three years to live!
What Jesus needed now was a team of men to help him.

This is to certify that Jesus of Nazareth has passed his test in resisting Satan's temptations.

Mark: 100%

DISCIPLES WANTED!

HAVE **YOU** GOT WHAT IT TAKES TO WORK ALONGSIDE ISRAEL'S MESSIAH? WE'RE LOOKING FOR TWELVE GOOD MEN AND TRUE TO LISTEN AND LEARN FROM THE MASTER. IF YOU DON'T MIND ROUGHING IT AND NOT EARNING A BEAN, THEN **THIS** IS THE JOB FOR **YOU**! MISFITS WELCOME! NO PREVIOUS EXPERIENCE NECESSARY!

APPLY NOW!

Er, not quite the approach we were looking for!
It happened more like this...

Jesus went throughout the region of Galilee and handpicked the twelve men that *he* wanted to help him. They were no doubt people Jesus had already impressed already so they didn't need much persuading.

This mixed bunch of fishermen, tax collectors and other sorts are what we call Jesus's disciples.

Now, with his twelve disciples in tow Jesus finally set about the job he'd been sent to do.

First stop the synagogue in Nazareth, (that's sort of the local Jewish church, if you didn't know).

Jesus stood up in front of the congregation, took the scroll with the Jewish scriptures on it and began to read.

THE SPIRIT OF THE LORD IS UPON ME BECAUSE HE HAS ANOINTED ME TO PREACH GOOD NEWS TO THE POOR. HE HAS SENT ME TO PROCLAIM FREEDOM FOR THE PRISONERS AND RECOVERY OF SIGHT FOR THE BLIND. TO RELEASE THE OPPRESSED. TO PROCLAIM THE YEAR OF THE LORD'S FAVOUR.

Then Jesus sat down.

Boring Bible Fact: Week in, week out, the Jewish people listened attentively as their scriptures (that was like their Bible) were read to out in their synagogues. The bit that Jesus read was written hundreds of years before and told the Jewish people what their Messiah was going to do when he arrived.

Now for the bombshell...

Or, to put it another way, Jesus was saying...

But the *bad* news was that nobody believed him.
In fact, they were furious!

They were so mad at Jesus that they tried to throw him off a cliff and kill him. Jesus had made his first enemies but this wasn't the last we've seen of them.

Next stop Capernaum...

This time Jesus got a better reception.

But there was more to Jesus than just what he had to say.
Jesus had been given the power and authority to attack anything
and everything to do with Satan.
That included evil spirits.
Because Satan wasn't like God he couldn't be in two places at
once so he used evil spirits to do his dirty work for him. *They*
were his evil army.
Whenever they got the chance to spoil someone's life they'd
jump at it.
Now their days were numbered.
They were no match for Jesus, God's Super Son...and they knew
it.

Showdown!

As Jesus walked into a synagogue in Capernaum an evil spirit
that was controlling a man shrieked at Jesus.

The evil spirit had no choice but to do what Jesus said.

Over the next three years Jesus healed thousands and thousands of people and did loads of miracles, not to impress people but to show them how much God cared for them.

SPOT THE MESSIAH Only someone with God's power could do such things!

Because Jesus spent so much time healing people, we know that God wants us to be well.

Jesus Heals A Paralysed Man

One day, while Jesus was in the middle of teaching a group of the Jewish religious leaders, some men arrived carrying their sick friend on a mat. The place was packed with people trying to listen to Jesus but they weren't deterred.

They climbed up on the roof, made a hole in it and then lowered the sick man down right in front of Jesus.

What do you think Jesus did?

a Told them off for disturbing him?
b Ignored the sick man?
c Apologised to the owner of the house for the roof being ruined?
d Healed the sick man?

You're right, it was d).

The Bible says that Jesus was impressed with their faith and healed their sick friend.

FRIEND, YOUR SINS ARE FORGIVEN.

WHO DOES HE THINK HE IS GOING AROUND FORGIVING SINS? ONLY GOD CAN DO THAT!

SPOT THE MESSIAH Jesus could have just told the man to get up and walk but he wanted the people of Israel to see that as God's Son he had the authority to forgive their sins as well!

When the paralysed man stood up, healed, the crowd were gobsmacked.

Jesus Feeds A Huge Crowd

Wherever Jesus went, vast crowds of people followed him, hanging on his every word or looking to get healed.

Such was the effect of Jesus on them that they often lost all track of time.

On one such occasion the disciples suddenly realised that night was drawing in...

Jesus didn't seem too concerned...

Just one small problem...

This didn't seem to worry Jesus in the slightest.
He got the crowd to sit down in groups and then, taking the
loaves and the fish in his hands he gave thanks to God for it.

Amazingly, there was enough food for everyone and more
besides.When the disciples had collected up all the broken
pieces they had another twelve basketfuls!

Fascinating Fact:

*The Bible says that the crowd was 5000 strong
not counting women and children which could make the
numbers up to something more like 10,000.*

**SPOT THE MESSIAH Jesus proved that not only did he have
power from God to do miracles but also that he had
compassion for people!**

Jesus Brings A Man Back To Life

Once, while Jesus was in Jerusalem, news reached him that his good friend, Lazarus, had died.

When he arrived at Bethany, where Lazarus had lived with his sisters, Mary and Martha, Jesus comforted them.

There was no doubt in Mary's mind that Jesus could have healed her brother, Lazarus, with just a word of command. I wonder whether she was ready for what happened next?

But what about the smell?! He'd been dead for **four days**!

Still wrapped in his grave clothes, Lazarus walked out of the tomb...very much alive!

SPOT THE MESSIAH Only someone with God's power could bring somebody back to life!

The Bible says that many of the onlookers put their trust in Jesus as their Messiah because of that awesome miracle...but not everyone.

Jesus was really beginning to get up the noses of the Jewish religious leaders.

Basically they were just plain jealous of him but they also knew that if people started to follow Jesus then their days might be numbered.

They weren't having that!

There was only one thing for it.

Jesus had to be eliminated, and the sooner the better!

Jesus performed so many healings and miracles even the Bible doesn't have enough room to record them all.

It wasn't only Lazarus that Jesus brought back to life, he did it a number of times. The Bible tells us that Jesus healed *every* sick person who came to him for healing and *every* kind of sickness. Other amazing things he did were walk on water, calm a violent storm with a word of command, turn water into wine, pay his taxes with a coin that a fish had swallowed and tell the disciples where to drop their fishing nets for a bumper miracle catch!

Now, let's take a look at some of the things Jesus had to *say*...

THE
TEACHINGS
OF
SUPER SON
(the juiciest
bits!)

Jesus Goes Up In The World

The only way that Jesus could get some time alone with his disciples, away from all the crowds, was by going up a mountain.

The disciples needed to be taught all they needed to know about being Jesus's followers.

GOD WILL BLESS YOU IF YOU ARE MEEK, HUMBLE AND PURE.

MAKE SURE YOU LIVE GOOD LIVES SO THAT PEOPLE CAN SEE THAT YOU LOVE GOD.

DON'T FORGET TO OBEY ALL OF GOD'S LAWS.

DON'T HOLD GRUDGES OR TAKE REVENGE. IN FACT, **LOVE** YOUR ENEMIES.

DON'T LEAVE YOUR WIFE.

DON'T SHOW OFF WHEN YOU DO GOOD DEEDS.

DON'T GET GREEDY FOR LOTS OF MONEY.

DON'T KEEP CRITICISING OTHERS UNTIL YOU'VE GOT YOUR OWN LIFE SORTED.

DON'T BE AFRAID TO ASK GOD FOR WHAT YOU NEED.

Jesus Tells Some Stories

When it came to teaching the crowds, Jesus used parables to get his point across.

Parables were short stories that had a special meaning.

You might be familiar with one or two of them...

The Lost Sheep

A man had 100 sheep but one day he discovered that one of them was missing.

After much searching the man found his lost sheep...

...and carried it back to the flock.

Jesus told that story to show them how happy God is when a lost sinner turns back to him.

The Wise Man and the Foolish Man

A foolish man decided to build a house.

So that's where he built his house.

A wise man decided to build a house.

With their houses built, the two men went inside to enjoy them. But a storm rose up and the house on the sand crumbled on its weak foundations while the house on the rock stayed firm.

Jesus told this parable about two men who had both listened to God's teachings but the foolish man had ignored them so when the time of trouble came, his life crumbled. The wise man, on the other hand, not only listened to God's teachings but built his life on them so that *nothing* could shake him.

Some Other Things That Jesus Taught

1 Love God with all your heart.
2 Love other people as much as you love yourself.
3 Trust God like a child does.
4 Don't look down on people.
5 Care for widows and poor people.
6 Be generous towards God.
7 Don't live your life around money.
8 Don't worry - trust God.

Just before we reach the finale of *Super Son* I think it's time we had a commercial break.
Did you know that the Bible is packed full of adverts?
You didn't?
Well that's because they're not called adverts in the Bible - they're called **prophecies**.

Prophecies are things that God
says to us through
people called 'prophets' -
they listen out for what God
has to say and then pass it on.
Like Isaiah...

Isaiah was one of a number of
prophets who told people that
a Messiah from God would
one day visit the earth.
Not only that but prophets
told people well in advance where the Messiah would be born,
what he would be like, some of things he would do and even
how people would treat him.

Like we said earlier in the book, if you wanted to check out
to see if a Messiah was for real or not then a bit of advance
warning or advertising would be really handy.

Here's a selection from hundreds of adverts (prophecies) that
you can find in the Bible...

COMING SOON TO THIS WORLD...

*'The virgin will be with child and will give birth to a son and will call
him Immanuel' (Which means God with us) - Isaiah 7:14*

If you remember, Jesus's mother Mary was a virgin!

*'But you, Bethlehem...out of you will come...one who will be ruler
over Israel' - Micah 5:2*

Jesus was born in Bethlehem.

'Then will the eyes of the blind be opened and the ears of the deaf unstopped. Then will the lame leap...and the mute tongue will shout for joy' - Isaiah 35:5

Jesus went about healing the blind, the deaf, the lame and the dumb.

And here's three more that you can check out as you read on...

'Rejoice greatly...Shout, Daughter of Jerusalem! See your king comes to you, righteous and having salvation, gentle and riding on a donkey, on a colt, the foal of a donkey' - Zechariah 9:9

'Even my close friend, whom I trusted, he who shared my bread, has lifted up his heel against me' - Psalm 41:9

'They divide my garments among them and cast lots for my clothing' - Psalm 22:18

Now back to the story!
This bit is like the finale...

THE SACRIFICE OF SUPER SON (mission accomplished!)

After three years on the road, teaching the Israelites about God and demonstrating God's love for them, the time had finally come for the big one.

Right from the word go, Jesus knew how the story would end which is why he was now headed right for Israel's capital city, Jerusalem.

The time for the final showdown had come.

Jesus was still as popular as ever among the crowds but the religious leaders were seething with anger and hatred towards him.

Everything that Jesus stood for infuriated them.

They'd long forgotten about loving and worshipping God.

What *they* loved most was keeping God's laws or more to the point, the hundreds and hundreds of extra ones they'd made up themselves.

Those man-made laws were the ones that Jesus seemed to have total disregard for and that's what really bugged the religious leaders.

The Bible says that as Jesus approached Jerusalem, he sent two of the disciples ahead to fetch a colt that had been prepared for him.

As Jesus rode the colt toward the great city the crowds spread their cloaks or palm branches on the road and shouted...

Remember the prophecy about a colt?

The next day, to everyone's horror, Jesus entered the Temple area and started to knock over the tables of the money-changers and the benches of those selling doves.

These people were exploiting those who came to offer sacrifices to God and had turned the place into nothing more than a rip-off market place.

As Jesus wandered through the Temple courts the religious leaders weren't far behind, muttering and grumbling to each other.

They were always on the lookout for ways to trick Jesus.

But Jesus was well aware that they were trying to trap him to either say something against the Roman rulers or against God.

Once again Jesus had outsmarted their scheming minds.

Time was moving on and Jesus knew that his days on earth were numbered.
As for the disciples they still hadn't cottoned on to what Jesus had been saying all along.
Time and time again he'd warned them that he would have to die but somehow they just didn't seem to listen.

This wasn't the case with everyone.

With the Jewish Passover feast just two days away and the religious leaders getting increasingly desperate for ways to arrest him, Jesus took some time out at the home of a man called Simon the Leper.

(Probably one of the many people suffering from the skin disease, leprosy, and whom Jesus had healed.)

While he reclined at the table a woman entered and poured expensive perfume over Jesus's head.

Jesus didn't think so.

LEAVE HER ALONE! SHE HAS DONE A BEAUTIFUL THING. THE POOR YOU WILL **ALWAYS** HAVE WITH YOU AND YOU CAN HELP THEM ANYTIME YOU WANT. BUT YOU WILL NOT ALWAY HAVE **ME**. SHE POURED PERFUME ON MY BODY TO PREPARE ME FOR MY BURIAL. WHEREVER THE GOOD NEWS ABOUT ME IS PREACHED THEN WHAT SHE HAS DONE WILL BE TOLD IN MEMORY OF HER.

Boring Bible Fact: Jesus was right! She's just had *another* mention, hasn't she?

One of the disciples, called Judas Iscariot, made a quick exit and headed off for a secret meeting with the religious leaders. At last they'd found someone to help them capture Jesus.

THIRTY PIECES OF SILVER TO BETRAY YOUR MASTER! CHEAP AT HALF THE PRICE!

Passover Time

If you read Boring Bible book *Magnificent Moses*
then you'll no doubt remember how God told the Israelites
(who were slaves in Egypt) to daub blood from a perfect and
unblemished sacrificed lamb around the door frames of their
houses. An angel from God was going to pass over all of Egypt
and kill the first born (that's the eldest child) to force them to
set the Israelites free. This was the final straw for Egypt's wicked
Pharaoh and he let the Israelites leave his land.
From then on, throughout all of Israel's history, year in, year
out, God had commanded the Israelites to remember how the
blood of a perfect lamb had saved them.

Jerusalem, being the capital city, must have been buzzing with
visitors who had come to celebrate the Feast of the Passover.
Jesus, being a Jew, was no exception.
He'd already made plans for a room to be prepared.

That evening, as Jesus and his twelve disciples reclined at the
table, the atmosphere must have been electric.
Even the triumphant entry into the city was a good indication
that something out of the ordinary was about to happen.

Remember the prophecy about the betrayal?

Before we go any further it wouldn't be a bad idea if we filled you in with some interesting info about what exactly went on in a Passover meal.

How To Hold A Passover Meal

Start off with a prayer to God.
Once you've done that, bless the cup of wine and pass it round.
Next, each person in the room takes herbs and dips them in salt water!
The head of the family then takes one of the flat cakes of unleavened bread (that's bread without yeast), breaks it and puts some aside.
If you're the youngest then you get to ask a question which is answered by the re-telling of the story of the very first Passover.

Now it's time to pass round cup of wine number two.

Before you all tuck in, everyone's got to wash their hands, thanks are given and the bread is broken.
Bitter herb dipped in sauce (no, not ketchup!) is passed round (that's when Judas is revealed as the betrayer).
The meal comes to its climax with some juicy roast lamb.
Jesus and his disciples had just finished this part of the Passover meal when Jesus surprised them all by breaking some of the bread, giving thanks and saying...

Then Jesus passed round a third cup of wine...

The disciples must have wondered what Jesus was saying.

It was as if he was telling them that God's old covenant (that's like a promise) with the Israelites was about to end and a new one begin.

The old covenant required the blood of a perfect lamb to be sacrificed to God to cover over the Israelites' sins.

Could it possibly be that Jesus was saying *he* was going to be sacrificed to God so that *his* blood could actually blot out their sins permanently?

While they sang a closing hymn, Judas slunk off to do his dirty deed.

The Big Build-Up

The disciples probably had no idea what was going to happen next but Jesus *definitely* did. Nothing that God ever does is an accident and Jesus knew full well what to expect as he and his motley group of followers headed out to the Mount of Olives.

It had been a busy day for Jesus and his disciples and their eyes were becoming heavy with tiredness.
I'll bet they were ready for their beds.

Not so fast.
You're a disciple aren't you?

Well I'm afraid *this* is more like the sort of bed you can expect!

It was a tough old life following Jesus around and not having anywhere to sleep was part of the package.

Jesus had always known that he would be put to death (that was part of God's plan), but now the thought of the pain he would have to endure tormented him.

To find his disciples asleep and completely oblivious to his suffering just made matters worse.

But the time for anguish was past.

Judas had arrived with the religious leaders and a crowd of armed men.

Cowardy Custard

The religious leaders had always been too cowardly and afraid to arrest Jesus while he was surrounded by the crowds of people who seemed to follow him wherever he went.

Now he was alone, they could finish the job.

All they wanted from Judas was to know which one was Jesus. (It was the dead of night and the darkness made it difficult to see.)

That was the signal they were waiting for.

Jesus didn't resist arrest but simply allowed himself to be captured.

The scared disciples started to fight back but when they realised that they were outnumbered they fled...just like Jesus had said they would.

Jesus was bundled off and taken to the home of Caiaphas, the High Priest. The religious leaders were determined to get Jesus for *some* crime or other *then* they could take him to be tried by the Roman governor.

As far as they were concerned, the sooner Jesus was out of the way, the better!

HE SAID HE COULD TEAR DOWN GOD'S TEMPLE AND REBUILD IT THREE DAYS LATER!

HE'S A TROUBLEMAKER!

HIS POWER COMES FROM SATAN!

HE BREAKS OUR LAWS!

HE **EVEN** HEALS ON THE SABBATH!

HE MIXES WITH SINNERS!

ARE YOU THE MESSIAH?

ARE YOU THE SON OF GOD?

This was Jesus's moment of truth.

If he said nothing he'd probably end up getting let off with a warning but if he admitted who he was then he would be signing his own death warrant.

Jesus had lit the blue touch paper, now watch those religious leaders explode...

Meanwhile, outside in the courtyard...

Suddenly a cock crowed and Peter remembered what Jesus had said about disowning him three times.

The Bible says that Peter wept at what he had done.

What Happened To Judas

Judas soon realised that he'd made a big mistake.

Although Jesus didn't live up to Judas's expectations of what a Messiah should be (such as perhaps getting rid of the Romans), there was no way he wanted him killed.

But it was too late.

The dastardly deed had been done and it was all *his* fault.

The Bible gives two accounts of what became of this traitor.

One of them says that he went back to the religious leaders and tried to convince them that Jesus was innocent.

When they told him that they didn't care he flung the 30 silver coins down at their feet and went off and hanged himself.

The other story says Judas used the money he'd got as payment and bought a field where he fell to his death. He burst open and his bowels spilt out.

Yuk!

And no, I'm not going to draw you a picture of it, it makes me feel all funny just *thinking* about it!

Back to the story...

While it was still early, Jesus was whisked off, in chains, and handed over to Pilate.

No, not *'pilot'* - **Pilate**. *Pontius* Pilate, the Roman governor.

But when Pilate tried to find out from Jesus what he was being accused of Jesus said...

...zilch!

One Last Chance

Pilate was at a loss to know what to do with Jesus.

He couldn't see that Jesus had done anything wrong.

Governing these Jews was a nightmare.

The last thing he needed was a riot on his hands.

Perhaps if he asked the crowd that had gathered what *they* wanted.

Pilate hadn't bargained on the jealous religious leaders stirring up the crowd.

For the record, Barabbas had rebelled against the Roman rulers and stood accused of murder and rioting.

Pilate could not get them to change their mind and Barabbas was freed.

Fascinating Fact:

Just in case you're wondering whether Pontius Pilate was a real person, archaeologists have discovered a piece of stone in a place called Caesarea that is inscribed with his name!

Although Jesus wasn't guilty of any crime, he was taken away to be executed.

Throughout history people have invented lots of different ways of executing people.

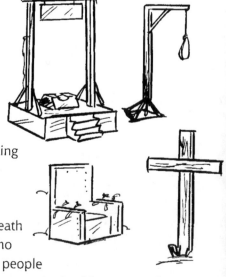

The Guillotine for cutting off heads - very popular during the French Revolution (unless it was your head!).

The Hangman's Noose for hanging people.

The Electric Chair for electrocuting criminals - still being used in the USA.

Crucifixion for a long, painful death - a favourite with the Romans who sometimes crucified hundreds of people at a time to deter rebellion by the people they'd conquered!

Before Jesus was crucified he was whipped and tortured by the Roman soldiers.

They beat Jesus over the head, spat on him and then pressed a crown made of sharp thorns onto his head.

The place where Jesus was going to be crucified was just outside the city.

Crucifixion involved being nailed through your hands or wrists (and sometimes your ankles) to a tree or a wooden cross.

It's impossible to imagine the excruciating pain those being crucified must have felt.

Boring Bible Fact: 'EXCRUCIATING' actually comes from the word crucify because it best describes the terrible pain.

Even though Jesus was now suffering the most awful agony he refused a drink containing the painkiller, myrrh.

Above Jesus's head the Romans had mockingly stuck a sign which read...

Passers-by hurled insults at him and taunted him.

The Bible tells us that the Roman soldiers passed their time dividing up Jesus's garments between them and then casting lots (gambling with dice) for his main piece of clothing, the tunic.

Remember the prophecy about casting lots for Jesus's clothing?

Nobody looking up at Jesus dying on that cross could possibly have realised what was going on before their very eyes.

From The Beginning Of Time

Right from the time Adam and Eve (the first people who ever lived) had rebelled (or sinned) against him, God had been

preparing a perfect human life to be sacrificed to wipe the slate clean and restore our friendship with him.

Now, a few thousand years on, the punishment the human race deserved for its sin was going to be taken by Jesus.

Jesus was *perfect* because he had been conceived by God but *human* because his birth mother was Mary.

Because God was fair and just, sin simply had to be punished. But if Jesus didn't step in and do something, not only couldn't we be friends again with God while we were alive, but when we died we wouldn't be allowed into heaven where God lives. Because God is full of mercy he doesn't want that to happen.

As God looked down from heaven, he saw his Son, Jesus, pouring his life out as a sacrifice for our sins.

Boring Bible Fact: Jesus is called 'the Lamb of God' because he was a sacrifice. At the very same time as he hung on that cross, lambs were being killed a stone's throw away in Jerusalem in preparation for the Passover Feast. God's timing was perfect!

Darkness

At noon, a most peculiar phenomenon occurred.
Suddenly, the whole country was covered
with darkness which the Bible says lasted
three hours.
It must have been terrifying.
But this wasn't just a cloudy day or an
eclipse.
An eclipse is when the moon passes in
front of the sun and blots out its light.

The Jewish Passover was always held at the time of a full moon
and when that happens the sun and moon are at completely
opposite sides of the sky, so it couldn't be that!

No, this was God in heaven making sure the world knew that this was his Son they were killing.

Fascinating Fact:

There are stories from other nations in Europe and Asia that also tell of a mysterious darkness that covered the land around this time in history. In some places they were even talking about it twenty years later!

While Jesus's mother Mary and many other friends looked on from a distance, Jesus cried out in a loud voice...

Then he bowed his head and died.

At that moment, according to the Bible, some strange things happened.

Without warning, the huge curtain that hung in the Temple and acted as a barrier between God and the people was torn in two.

SPOT THE MESSIAH This was a sign from God that, because Jesus had taken the punishment for our sin, the way was now open for us to be his friends again.

Then an earthquake shook the ground...

Boring Bible Fact: Christians call the day that Jesus died 'Good Friday' because they know that when Jesus cried out "It is finished" it meant he had succeeded in sorting sin once and for all. And that *is good*!

The Bible tells us that Jesus was laid in a tomb donated by a wealthy man called Joseph of Arimathea.

With Jesus's mother Mary, and Mary Magdalene, (another of Jesus's followers), looking on, a large stone was rolled across the entrance to the tomb.

Next day, the religious leaders started to get the jitters.
They were starting to get worried that Jesus's disciples might come and nick the body and pretend that Jesus had risen from the dead.

Pilate *also* didn't want any more trouble.
He wasted no time in dispatching Roman soldiers to guard the tomb until the third day.
To make doubly certain there was no funny business they even put a seal on the tombstone so that they'd know if anyone had so much as touched it.
The day after Jesus had been executed was a Jewish Sabbath (Saturday), which was a day of rest.

Jesus's mother and Mary Magdalene had been keen to take spices to put on Jesus's dead body as was the custom.
So, early on Sunday morning the two women hurried off to the tomb.

Boring Bible Interesting Thought: I wonder if they had considered how they were actually going to prepare Jesus's body when there was a whopping great tombstone blocking the way? Just a thought!

As things turned out they didn't have to worry.
Someone was about to do it for them.

There was a violent earthquake (two in two days is becoming a bit of a habit), and an angel from God appeared before them.

I KNOW YOU ARE LOOKING FOR JESUS WHO WAS CRUCIFIED. HE ISN'T HERE, HE HAS BEEN RAISED JUST AS HE SAID.

FAINT!

The angel had rolled away the stone for them.

Mary and Mary peeked into the tomb but all that was left were the linen cloths that Jesus had been wrapped in.

Before they'd had the chance to run far, Jesus appeared to them.

In fact, the Bible tells us that Jesus appeared to more than **500** people (including the disciples), on a number of occasions, for 40 days.

First of all, some of them couldn't believe their eyes but there was no doubt about it, it was Jesus, come back to life - but not like Lazarus, whom Jesus brought back to life.

Jesus had been transformed and given a *new* sort of body which was designed for heaven because he would soon be going back to his Father in heaven.

There was one disciple whom Jesus made a special point of spending time with.

It was Simon Peter. (He was originally just called Simon but Jesus gave him the extra name, Peter, which means 'rock'.)

He was the one who'd denied having anything to do with Jesus but Jesus was giving him a second chance.

Do you see what Jesus was doing?
Three times Simon Peter had denied knowing Jesus.
And *three times* he'd now said he loved him.
The damage was undone!

On a hillside overlooking Galilee, Jesus and his eleven remaining
disciples met together one last time.

Jesus had one last instruction for his disciples...

DO NOT LEAVE JERUSALEM BUT WAIT FOR THE GIFT MY FATHER PROMISED. IN A FEW DAYS THE HOLY SPIRIT WILL COME UPON YOU AND YOU WILL BE FILLED WITH POWER AND YOU WILL BE WITNESSES FOR ME IN JERUSALEM, JUDEA, SAMARIA AND TO THE ENDS OF THE EARTH.

And with that, before their very eyes, Jesus was taken up into heaven.

As far as Jesus is concerned, that wasn't the end of the story, just the *beginning*.

Here are some of the promises that Jesus made while he lived on earth.

THERE ARE MANY ROOMS IN MY FATHER'S HOUSE AND I AM GOING TO PREPARE A PLACE FOR YOU.

EVERYONE WHO BELIEVES IN ME WILL NOT DIE BUT HAVE ETERNAL LIFE.

MY PURPOSE IS TO GIVE YOU LIFE.

IF ANYONE DECLARES PUBLICLY THAT HE BELONGS TO ME, I WILL DO THE SAME FOR HIM BEFORE MY FATHER IN HEAVEN.

I WILL BE WITH **YOU** ALWAYS.

I WILL COME AGAIN.

IF YOU BELIEVE, YOU WILL RECEIVE WHATEVER YOU ASK IN PRAYER.

Jesus promised that one day he would return to the earth to declare an end to Satan's rule.

But he won't be coming back as a baby this time but as a mighty king with an army of angels from heaven.

Boring Bible Fact: There are an amazing 1846 references in the Bible to Jesus coming back again to the earth.

Until that time Jesus had left the disciples in charge to continue his work of getting people out of Satan's kingdom and into *his* kingdom.

That's what our next Boring Bible book, *Hyper Holy Happenings* is all about so if you want to find out some of the amazing things that happened right after Jesus had gone back to heaven then you'll need to buy yourself a copy.

How Can We Be Sure That Jesus Was A Real Person?

Some people say that Jesus was just a made up person and that he didn't really exist.

Well, that's not what people who lived around that time thought.

The Roman rulers had historians to keep a written record of what was going on throughout the Roman Empire.

A man called **Tacitus** wrote this about the followers of Jesus in around AD52...

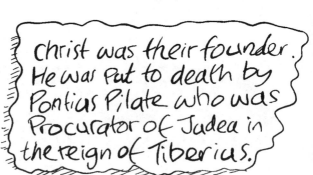

Christ was their founder. He was put to death by Pontius Pilate who was Procurator of Judea in the reign of Tiberius.

Boring Bible Fact: Christ was just another title that people used when talking about Jesus. All it meant was 'anointed'. 'Christ' wasn't Jesus's surname!

And then there was **Josephus**, the Jewish historian.

Now there was, about this time, Jesus, a wiseman...he was a doer of wonderful works, a teacher of such men... He was the Christ and when Pilate, at the suggestion of principal men among us, condemned him to the cross. Those that loved him at first did not forsake him. He appeared to them alive again on the third day...

Serapion had a thing or two to say...

...what advantage did the Jews gain from executing their wise King (Jesus)?

And other *Jewish* historians also mention him...

> ## On the eve of the Passover they killed the Nazarene.

Not forgetting **Thallus** and **Phlegon** who tried to explain away the great darkness that came over the land during Jesus's crucifixion.

So what do **you** think?
Was Jesus the Messiah?
If he was then that means that the Son of God's visit to the earth 2000 years ago can change your life...if you want it to.
It is estimated that **2 billion** people (that's one third of the world's population), have accepted God's offer to have their sins wiped out by Jesus.
Are you one of them?

Have a quick look at some of the people's lives Jesus changed while he was on the earth and then maybe you'll want to join them.

Matthew
Nobody loved him because he was a tax collector for the Romans.
Jesus made him one of his disciples and proved that he cared for everybody, however rotten they were.

The leper

Israelites with the dreaded skin disease, leprosy, were outcasts

but Jesus healed many. When he touched them he showed that he accepted them.
One healed leper came back to thank Jesus because his life had been changed.

An adulterous woman

The Israelites had a law that a women who wasn't faithful to her

husband and had sex with another man should be stoned to death.
When this lady came before Jesus he forgave her sin and gave her a second chance.

If **you** want a second chance to be friends again with God it's as simple as thanking Jesus for taking the punishment for your sin, telling God you're sorry for doing wrong and then asking him to forgive you.

But being one of Jesus's followers isn't for cowards.

Jesus expects his followers to live lives that make God happy. That means being kind and generous, loving and forgiving people, reading the Bible and talking to God regularly, (well that's a few things for starters).

It'll also mean you'll need to get stuck into a local church that you like so you can meet together with other Christians who follow Jesus.

Just in case you're thinking that this seems like hard work then relax.

When you let Jesus be No.1 in your life he promises to send his Holy Spirit to come and live inside you to encourage you and to prove that it's for real.

Sound good?

Then why not go for it...it'll be the best decision you could ever make.

Oh, yes, and why not draw yourself into the box below to include yourself in with the people whose lives Jesus has changed!

The Bit at the end

Just before we leave, here's a reminder of some of the stuff that we've been looking at...

What's Been Happening?

The Israelites have been patiently waiting for a Messiah.

At long last, Jesus is born.

Lots of visitors (including angels).

Jesus grows up (but no family photos for us to look at).

Jesus is finally launched as God's Messiah (baptism and temptations).

Disciples are signed up.

Lots of healings and miracles.

Lots of teaching (sometimes in parables).

Lots of enemies (the religious leaders).

Jesus catches a donkey into Jerusalem.

Jesus and disciples eat Passover feast (their last meal together).

Jesus arrested and tried.

Jesus crucified.

Jesus laid in a tomb.

The empty tomb (Jesus has risen from the dead).

Jesus appears to hundreds of people.

Jesus goes back up into heaven.

A Reminder Of The Main Characters

Mary and Joseph.

Loads of angels.

Jesus.

Shepherds (and not forgetting their sheep).

Wise men.

Herod (*not* such a wise man!).

John (the baptist).

Religious leaders (boo, hiss!).

The twelve disciples.
Pontius Pilate.
And, last but not least, all those crowds who kept popping up all over the place.

Now, over to you!
Write down which bits of the Bible that you don't find boring any more...

One more thing. How about getting your hands on a *real* Bible so you can check all the brill stuff that we didn't have space to include in this book. There are lots of great versions that are just for kids.
Have fun!

HERE ARE SOME BITESIZE -BITS- OF THE BIBLE

(JUST TO GIVE YOU A TASTE OF A **REAL** BIBLE!)

GO ON — HAVE A NIBBLE!

For God loved the world so much that he gave his only Son, so that everyone who believes in him may not die but have eternal life.

John 3: 16

CHEW!

SLURP!

CHOMP!

Jesus answered him. "I am the way, the truth, and the life; no one goes to the Father except by me."
John 14: 6

(Jesus said)..."I have come in order that you might have life – life in all its fullness."

John 10: 10

CHEW!

CHOMP!

MUNCH!

Jesus drew near and said to them, "I have been given all authority in heaven and on earth. Go, then, to all peoples everywhere and make them my disciples: baptize them in the name of the Father, the Son and the Holy Spirit, and teach them everything I have commanded you. And I will be with you always, to the end of the age."

Matthew 28: 18 - 20

SLURP!

NIBBLE!